# Mission Possible:

# How To Get Your House Ready For Sale In 30 Days

D1404002

Also by Norah Deay

**Non-Fiction**

How to Become The Go To Person

**Fiction**

**Novella**

Coming Home To Murder - #1 in Cozy Mystery series

**Short Stories**

Imagine

Choices

No Dogs Allowed

Fame and Misfortune


If you enjoy this book and find it useful, please leave a review.

Reviews encourage other readers to buy the book

# Contents

## Introduction

As a Personal Assistant, I've worked in the real estate industry for over 10 years, full-time and part-time and have first-hand knowledge of the stress people are under when they've to get their house ready for sale. I've done it twice and will never do it again without a plan. The *How to Get Your House Ready to Sell In 30 Days* plan.

We've all watched TV shows about decluttering – it easily was the house-and-home word of the 2000s – but until you're faced with shifting 20 years of your life that's been packed into a 3-bed house, you don't know the reality.

This guide will take you step-by-step through your home over 30 days and you will end up with a house any buyer will want. More importantly, a house that's sparkling, tidy and in great condition is always going to achieve a better monetary outcome than its tired and grubby neighbor.

Any money you spend will be recouped in the sale price but unless you have some serious issues with your roof, electrical wiring or your foundations are falling in, this plan is not going to cost much money at all. The only thing you will need in abundance is **elbow grease** (i.e. strenuous physical exertion).

So, block out 30 days in your calendar because you're going to be entirely focused on getting your old house ready, so you can move on to your new house.

# Day 1 – How do Buyers see my House?

When you put your home on the market you are signing up to the third (after death and divorce) most stressful situation you'll ever have to deal with. Especially when you realize that buyers are not seeing your pride and joy; they are seeing your *property,* their potential home, with a very critical eye. But, remember one thing; you are not alone! It's a difficult process but I can help.

For the next 30 days, you will be guided through the process of "staging" your house for a quick sale. This is just another way to say you are going to make YOUR house the jewel of the real estate market in your neighborhood. But, before you dig in, take a deep breath. Let it out. You have a lot of work to do in the next 30 days to get your home ready. You will need a clear head and a strong constitution, but YOU CAN DO IT. Let's get started!  But first, a dose of reality.

## Reality vs The Dream

The first thing to know is that the house we are currently living in is much different to the *idea* of the house we want to buy. As house buyers, we are picky and have visions of neat perfection. We may live with life's clutter in our own house, but when we go shopping for a new house, we expect neat, tidy, and uncluttered.

But, the truth is that we have busy lives and we have to live in our house. We end up with piles of shoes in the hallway, laundry baskets overflowing, and our kitchen benchtops littered with small appliances like little gastronomic soldiers. *But we must live here, we cry.* Is this so wrong?  The awful truth is, yes. When you are staging your house to sell, clutter is a deal-breaker. Is that harsh?  Yes. Is it true?  Definitely.

To make your house as marketable and attractive as possible, you need to match the buyer's expectations. To you, unless you already live in a pristine, clutter-free home, this may mean some big changes. So, where do you start?  By learning more about what a buyer wants.

## Your Mission

To get a sense of just how far apart a buyer's dream is from your reality, visit a few open homes in your asking range and style of property (don't visit a four-bedroom country house if you're selling a two-bedroom townhouse). DO visit a few show homes where you can get an idea of what buyers are expecting these days. You may not be able to replicate exactly but you'll pick up a few ideas.

Take notes. What were your first impressions?  What struck you about this house the moment you saw it?  Was it the garden?  The sparkling windows?  The pristine paintwork or the Triple garage?  Or, might it be the missing mailbox, the dead pot plants or the peeling paint? Whatever it was, jot it down, good or bad.

Once inside, again, write down your first thoughts. Do the rooms appear airy and spacious or dark and dingy? If the décor doesn't appeal to you can it be easily changed? Do you feel relaxed and comfortable as you walk around or are you afraid to move in case you damage something or worse, pick up a germ or a million?

As a buyer, what impresses you, and what distresses you?  What would you do differently if it was your house? You need to know this before you start staging your own home. Knowledge is power and knowing what a buyer is looking for is exactly what it takes to sell your house.

That's Day 1 over and you know what you must do. Get a good night's sleep because tomorrow is going to be a busy day.

# Day 2 – Create Clutter-Free Closets

One of the first things buyers notice in a house is space. We're talking about not only square meterage, but closets and other storage. Remember how spacious everything looked in the show homes? You want to replicate the same feeling in your house because a buyer wants space. You may be thinking it's okay to leave your things stuffed in the closets, there's no problem. Yes, there is. Visualization - that's the problem.

You need potential buyers to think they will have oodles of storage space if they buy your house. Of course, making the closets larger isn't normally an option, but you can make them *appear* larger. Again, visualization is everything. How does one accomplish this optical illusion? By making it appear as if your closets still have plenty of space available to be filled.

## Your Mission

Today you're going to declutter your closets. How? Well, as difficult as this may seem, the plain fact is you need to get rid of your stuff.

Don't panic. I'm not asking you to throw away anything. If you want to keep your treasures, go right ahead. If your collection of old picture frames makes you happy, keep them. But you have to get it all out of sight while your house is on the market.

This may require some pre-planning on your part, depending on how much stuff you must stash. Perhaps you will need to stock up on boxes or plastic bins. I'm a big fan of plastic bins. They can be stacked and used as moving boxes when the time comes. If you don't want to spend money, a popular place to get good sturdy boxes, that are the right size to handle easily, is at a liquor store. They are free and small enough to lift and move around.

Once you have the boxes, you will need a place to put them. If you have storage that's convenient, use that. A temporary storage unit may be worth the few dollars it costs in return for a successful sale. If you have one spare room, a pile of boxes hidden behind a decorative screen is less distracting than a pile of junk stuffed in a closet taking up precious space.

Now that you have something to store your stuff in and somewhere to put it, it's time to crack on. Start with the easiest closets first. How about the hall closet? Your hall closet should contain nothing more than a couple of seasonal coats, a pair of boots or two, some accessories, and a few nice-looking hangers. Nothing else. Be sure the floor is practically bare and you can see all four walls and the ceiling.

The less stuff you have in your closets, the better. It's all about empty space. Repeat the same process for linen and utility closets. Sort out anything that is not necessary and store it.

Now for the bedrooms. This might be a bit more difficult. Here you need to remove everything. Yes, Everything. Cull your clothing to about a dozen outfits. Arrange them by color and hang them up neatly on matching hangers. Yes, make your clothes sparse and match the hangers. Seem silly? It won't to a buyer. Box up anything and everything that is not currently being worn. You can keep a few boxes on high shelves and the floor can accommodate a few pairs of shoes, but when a potential buyer opens the door, they should be left with a feeling of space.

Make sure each closet is no more than half full. You want to create the illusion of space. If the buyer opens a closet door and narrowly misses being hit on the head by a falling shoebox (it happens) they will know immediately that they will never get all their stuff in that space.

So, pack it up and get it out of there. Your closets need to scream "Look at all the room in here!" Without that, a potential buyer will walk away and never look back. Get busy and get this very important decluttering chore done today so you can move on to the next step. See you tomorrow!

# Day 3 – Pack and Purge the Junk Room

Which room is your dumping ground? I know you have one. Everyone does. Yours might be the basement, the guest room, your office, or the laundry room. Or maybe you just call it what it is – the Junk Room.

Today is the day that your junk room' bites the dust. The phrase for today is "pack and purge." Repeat it out loud; "pack and purge." This is your mantra. It will get you through the day. What does today's mantra mean? It's time to find out.

## Your Mission

Everyone has flotsam and jetsam in their daily life. You know what it is. It's the stuff that you stick away in the room you have designated a dumping ground, until you can get to it, read it, sew it, write it, color it, paint it, fix it, sign it, cook it, etc. etc. You may have stuck it in this room because you didn't know what to do with it at the time. Well, today it has a place, and that place is out of sight, and NOT in this room.

Yes, it is time to pull out those boxes and bins again. It's time to "pack and purge." Start in any corner of your 'junk room' and pull everything out. Don't take time to think about the items you have; just pull them out. Now, label three boxes - keep, give, toss. Sit down and begin putting everything in one of those three boxes. Don't think too hard; you can always go back if you have time to sort later. If you can't decide what to do with an item immediately, just put it in the 'keep' box and don't worry about it right now.

The idea here is to box it all up so your room is clear. Once you have gathered your flotsam and jetsam, move the boxes out to a secure storage place. Now, organize and clean your 'junk room' and turn it back into the room it's intended to be.

You want the room to match the appealing description on the listing, don't you? Imagine this room from a realtor's viewpoint. Could you really expect your realtor to show your house with a description of "mystery room" or "junk room?" How would you explain the embarrassing picture of this room with its piles of junk to a potential buyer? How would you feel about pictures of your junk plastered all over the internet? Will those pictures help sell your house?

You know the answer. This may be a tedious process, but consider this; every piece of junk you put in a box is worth money – real money –

when you get that first offer from a buyer who has been dazzled with that guest room of yours!

Pack and Purge.. Pack and Purge. Sounds a lot better now, doesn't it? Tomorrow you can tackle something a bit smaller. See you then!

# Day 4 – A Pleasant Pantry Sells

Your kitchen's pantry deserves a day all to itself. You need your pantry to look huge and, yes, inviting. If your house is meant for family living and lots of big meals, your pantry should express this. If your house is all about making small spaces work, get creative with your pantry. Some houses have big walk-in pantries, while others have a single door linen closet size. Still other houses have a bank of cupboards that are used for food storage. You may even split your pantry between food items and other necessary kitchenware, even brooms and mops.

Whatever your kitchen offers, the buyer wants to see the potential. You have two objectives here, so you really need to dig in up to your elbows with this task. Get ready for a full day.

## Your Mission

If you have more than one kitchen pantry, just pick one to start with. Get out your sturdy boxes, bins, and your rubbish bin. Open your pantry and start by taking everything off the shelves. Do this methodically, taking one item off the shelf, decide if it's edible, then either put it in a box to keep, or throw it out. During this process you will run into food items that you will never eat, but that are perfectly fine. Label one box for charity (City Mission is always looking for non-perishables) and put those items in there.

Once you have sorted your food items into boxes, fill a bucket with clean water and gentle soap. Wipe down all the shelves, walls, and the doors. Now, with a dry or slightly damp clean cloth, pick each item you are keeping out of the box, wipe it off, and set it in the pantry. But keep in mind your end result. Imagine you are creating a display at the Container Store or a supermarket shelf. Group like items together and leave space between the groups. Line up all the cans so that the labels face the same way.

If you have attractive containers, fill those with your pasta rather than having half filled bags with twist ties. Smaller items should be grouped in nice baskets or decorative containers. And make sure there is absolutely no food items on the floor. That immediately tells your potential buyer that you don't have enough room on the shelves. Don't let your pantry spill over into your kitchen anywhere.

Remember, you are trying to make your pantry look roomy. It should appear there is plenty of room to fill when a new owner moves in. Putting everything in neat rows, consolidating small items, and having everything shiny clean will help give the buyer a 'fresh' look at your kitchen's pantry. If you have an area in your kitchen where you store cleaning or paper items, be sure to separate that from the food. Think about investing in a hanging system for the broom and mop, and storage systems for paper products like aluminum foil, plastic wrap, spare plastic bags, or other necessities. And don't forget those appliances that you won't be using any time soon. Get that pasta maker, ice cream machine, and bread maker out of the pantry and into a box for storage. Remember, if your pantry looks crowded, it tells the buyer there isn't enough room!

You want your pantry to have lots and lots of air space. It can also be pretty. If you have a walk-in pantry, for instance, think about hanging artwork on the back wall. A still life, like Andy Warhol's Campbell's Soup would be a nice touch but anything food-related would work. Your pantry shelves can be pretty, too. Buy some pretty oils and vinegars (but only if you would actually use them.) Think of your pantry as a little jewel box to show off your delicious food. You want it to be remembered; not just for how clean it is, but for something intangible, perhaps. You want a buyer to walk into every other house thinking, "This is okay, but that one pantry we saw was so cute and so roomy." That's YOUR pantry they'll be talking about, but only if you do the work.

Your kitchen's appearance starts from the inside out. The things a buyer will remember about your kitchen begins with a feeling – a feeling of space and quality. If your pantry stands out in these ways, that potential buyer will be haunted by it, and that's what you want. This was a big task, I know. But, as you see the house shape up, you'll gain momentum each day. Now you are ready to move on to the rest of the kitchen. Get some rest and get ready for tomorrow.

# Day 5 – Get Your Kitchen Down To Basics

Now that your pantry is beautiful, close the door, turn around, and take a look at the rest of the kitchen. What do you see? You probably see a room that works hard all the time, day in and day out. This is a room that gets a lot of wear and tear. This is a room that not only gets dirty, but it collects all the moments of our lives. Just take a look at what you have on the refrigerator door. Look at the windowsills, the counter-tops, the walls, and the top of the refrigerator. Do you see what I mean?

This room is LIVED IN! Let me put it this way: If aliens landed in your kitchen they would learn everything they need to know about you and your family with one look. This is a big task. There's no way around it. But, you can approach it in a step-by-step manner to make the job a bit easier. Let's begin.

**Your Mission**

Okay, it's time to tackle one of the hardest things you will do today. It's time to get all that stuff off the refrigerator. Strip it bare. Yes, that means you have to take off every last magnet, picture, and all those precious little drawings your kids and grandkids made. I know you love it all, but it needs to go away for a while. Why? Because YOU love it... your potential buyer does NOT. You want your refrigerator to be a pure, stark landscape. In fact, this one simple task can change the whole feeling of space and order when a buyer first walks into your kitchen. Put all those goodies away safe and sound. Take a deep breath, and move on.

The walls are next. Do you have a bulletin board? How about a calendar? Do you have a collection of coffee cups? Do you have a knick-knack shelf? If you have any of these things, you need to take them down. If you need something to function, like a calendar, put it behind a door. Pack up your lovely collections and knick-knacks for your next house.

Now, take a look at your bench-tops. What do you see? If it's more than one or two items, you have too much. Yes, a buyer expects to see a few things on the bench-tops. Your Nespresso and a cookie jar are nice. Maybe even a nice knife block and a pretty cutting board are okay. But if you add to that a blender, toaster, food processor, mixer, dish drainer, cooking utensils, can opener, canisters, paper towels, spoon rest, salt and pepper.... whew! Well, you see what I mean.

These food preparation items may all be necessary, which makes it very difficult to put this stuff away. But, if you think this is impossible to do, consider this: Every item you leave on your counter reduces the sale price of your home. Do you REALLY want to leave out the blender? What are you willing to pay to have that blender on the counter, because it could easily cost you. A clean slate in the kitchen invites the buyer to move in, get comfortable, look around. Makes you think, doesn't it?

Of course, you'll want to look around the floors, too. Pick up the rugs and expose a cleanly scrubbed floor. Take any extra chairs or stools out to the garage. Again, you want the buyer to see a wide-open room with lots of space. Now that the most noticeable surfaces are swept clean, you'll need to make sure your cupboards are relatively bare inside, too. Of course, you can't be expected to clear out all your dishes and pots and pans. However, you want to strip down things to whatever comfortably fits into your space.

When a potential buyer looks in your cupboards, be sure the items in there follow this simple rule: a place for everything and everything in its place. This order, combined with lots of airy space, gives the impression of lots and lots of room. Your organized cupboards should be about half-full when you're done. The less stuff in the cupboards, the more spacious they look. Just like your closets. See a theme here? You want a buyer to walk out of your kitchen thinking about the incredible space, not how crowded the kitchen was or about the lack of bench-space.

Yes, it's a pain to clear out and live without all your stuff. This is the stuff you are used to. But, a buyer doesn't love your stuff and never will. It looks like clutter to a buyer.

Want to sell your house fast? Turn your kitchen into the kitchen your BUYER wants, instead of your kitchen. When you take a look at your kitchen and think; "This isn't MY kitchen!" you are on the right track. Once this difficult task is completed, you will be well on your way to gaining the momentum you need to move on.

This was a hard day so go get some rest. I'll meet you back here tomorrow.

# Day 6 – Cook Up a Sale with a Shiny Clean Stove

Today we have a small project, in that it doesn't cover much in the way of space. However, this is a big job that many people put off doing. Most stoves only have a few elements to consider – the burners and pans, the surface, and the area with the knobs. Then the oven contains the racks, three walls, and the door.

Regardless of what sort of stove top and oven combination you have, there are a few cleaning strategies to consider. So, let's get started giving this hard-worker a fresh new look.

**Your Mission**

Before you dig in with cleansers and scrubbers, you have to know what sort of oven and stove top you are cleaning. You may want to grab your owner's manual to double check if you are not sure.

**Oven cleaning tips:** If you no longer have the owner's manual, you can pretty much figure your oven fits into one of three categories: regular surface, continuous cleaning surface, and self cleaning surface. You'll need to figure out which one you have before you decide what cleaner you can use. If you have a regular (smooth) surface oven, you can use oven cleaners such as the foam spray-on type, if you wish. If you prefer to avoid the chemical cleaners, a good scrubbing with a mild soap and water, baking soda, or vinegar and water will get the job done.

Use a small scrubbing brush if you need to loosen burned on grease, rinse with clear water or add a bit of vinegar to help cut the soap residue, too. Continuous cleaning and self cleaning models have special surfaces that most manufacturers warn against using harsh cleaners on. Now, if your continuous cleaning oven has actually kept itself clean, you may only need to wipe the inside surfaces with a wet rag just to make it perfectly clean. These ovens may deposit a bit of ash or powder on the bottom and around the edges, so just wipe those up. If you have a large spill, you may want to soak it with a vinegar and baking soda paste, then wipe up with a clean rag.

If you use the self cleaning function on your oven, just be sure to wipe up the pile of ash and follow up with a clean rag soaked in vinegar and water to freshen the entire surface. Don't forget to wash up the racks, broiler pan, and to wipe out any storage drawer you might have under the oven. And don't forget to clean and shine the oven door, inside and out.

**Stove top cleaning tips:** As for the stove top, there again you have many types to consider. If you have a gas stove, you would probably have burner "grates" to lift off and soak. Remove any drip pans under the burner grates and soak them in a sink of soapy water. If they are beyond repair (rusted, dented, stained) replace them. They are cheap enough and they make a real impact in the appearance of the stove top. Do NOT wrap aluminum foil around the pans under the burners. It looks sloppy and says "I'm hiding some terrible stuff from you" to the buyer. Buy new pans. If you can't get the pans that match your stove, buy real aluminum liners made to put on top of your stove top's drip pans.

Electric stoves may either have heating coils with drip pans underneath or they may be a smooth surface. Again, be sure to take apart as much as you can so you can clean everything carefully. If you have a smooth surface, be sure to choose a cleaner that is appropriate to avoid scratches. If you have stuck on food, it's better to soak for a few minutes rather than take the risk of scratching with a scrubber. You can remove an electric burner 'coil' from the stove top and wipe it off with a damp paper towel. Don't soak them in the sink, just wipe them off.

Now give the entire stove surface a wipe down to remove any food splotches and grease. Shine up everything! Don't forget that door front again. Wash the knobs, switches, dials and everything. Stand back and take a look. If something doesn't shine, clean it again. Your oven and stove top must be perfectly clean to keep potential buyers looking. Don't give them something as silly as a dirty stove as an excuse to walk away

# Day 7 – Knick Knack No-No

You're at the end of the first week. Doesn't that make you feel good?  It should!  You are getting closer to your goal of having a perfectly staged house that will bring you the best possible price.

Today is one of the hardest days you will have while preparing your house for sale. Why?  Because your house is your home and your home reflects your personality and showcases the people and things you love. Just look around. You probably have portraits and pictures of the family. You also probably have drawings from the kids posted proudly.

Not everyone appreciates your collection of dolls, ducks, elephants, thimbles, gnomes, flamingos, or what have you. I know it's hard to believe, but it's true. It's not personal, so don't get offended. You probably wouldn't like their precious pieces either. So, it's time to brace yourself and take a hard look at what you've got sitting around your house. I warned you this wouldn't be easy, so take a deep breath, and begin.

## Your Mission

Remember first, this is not about design, taste, or anything personal. It's about a clean slate!  There's only one way to make your house desirable to a potential buyer and that's to give the buyer possibilities. A buyer dreams of nothing but possibilities when they arrange to see a house. If every surface is covered with your stuff, a buyer can't imagine their stuff there.

You're going to need some more boxes and bins. You might as well start with the walls and remove all your family pictures – yes all of them. Wrap them up, pack them away, or take them to your office. Just remove them from your house. Continue walking through the house, removing family pictures from the walls and packing them up. If you have a large landscape or other generic print, leave it. You are not stripping your house totally of all décor, just of your personal items.

Look now at any bookcases, tables, and other surfaces. If you have a collection of small snapshots, family pictures, religious items, or other knick-knacks, box them up. Again, there's nothing personal about this. If you have a mantlepiece, reduce the décor to a couple of candles or a vase or two. Windowsills need to be completely clean, too, so take a trip through the house and gather, gather, gather.

I know all these chores today are difficult emotionally. That's why this job requires an opinion from someone outside of the family. Bring in a friend and ask them to look at your house, like a buyer. No excuses. No arguments. If he or she tells you the silk flower arrangements over the doors must go, or snickers at your All Blacks collection, or your beautiful draperies are way too heavy, get rid of them.

Once this day is over, you will need a hot bath and some pampering. It's a tough day, but will pay off in the end. The faster you sell, the faster you can unwrap all your favorite knick knacks and family pictures. It will all work out just fine!

# Day 8 – Strip Your Bathroom Bare

It's the start of a new week and you may not be as enthusiastic as you were last week. Now is not the time to be faint-hearted. You decluttered a lot last week and today is another purging and packing day. The rooms you are tackling today are usually the smallest in the house – the bathrooms.

Is that cupboard under the sink a bit unsightly? Are the medicine cabinets crowded with out-of-date medications? Are the drawers housing stains and leaks from things you don't want to know about? And what about the bath and shower?

You know what you have to do, but we'll just take a look so you don't miss anything.

## Your Mission

Buyers believe, and rightly so, that they have 'carte blanche' to look into every nook and cranny of your house, even your bathrooms. They have already looked in all your closets, cupboards, and under the beds. So, why not the bathrooms?

Believe it or not, buyers are looking for reasons NOT to buy your house. They are heavily invested in the process of elimination. Going from house to house, buyers are anxious to eliminate as many houses as possible from their list of possibilities. It's just easier that way.

Imagine a buyer coming into your bathroom and seeing rust stains on the bath or a soap-scum-coated shower door. Now, granted, it may not be a deal breaker, but it will move your house from the "amazing" list to the "have to come up with a really good reason to look at this house again" list.

You might as well begin with the bathtub and shower. This is the area that catches a lot of the clutter and grime. Gather up the piles of bottles, back scrubbers, and bath toys and throw it all in a bin and set aside. Your bathtub must be empty, clean, and pristine. Now scrub, scrub, scrub until the area is sparkling like a gem.

The toilet needs a good scrubbing from top to bottom, not just the bowl. And, if you have a cover on the toilet lid and/or seat, get rid of it. You want your bathroom to say "clean and germ free" and those covers, no matter how cute, do NOT say clean, or germ free. Save them for your new house.

*Tip: If you have old toothbrushes don't throw them out just yet.*

Now empty out under the sink, the medicine cabinet, any closets, cupboards, shelves, or drawers. Put it all in bins and set aside. Now scrub everything until it sparkles and squeaks. You may also want to use this time to wash or replace your shower curtain, window coverings, rugs, and even your towels. Find a new out-of-sight place for your toilet plunger and brush. All those necessities you've thrown in bins can now be sorted into convenient carry-all bins and stored away behind closed doors. Put a carry-all bin together for each family member so everyone has what they need in one place. And more importantly, they can hide their stuff away again after using it.

You have a clean slate now in the bathroom. Go ahead and add decorative towels and pretty soap. Remember the show homes? That's the bathroom you are aiming for here. Everything must be presentable and pretty. Besides being clean, why did I have you strip the bathroom bare? Even in the bathrooms, you need to give the impression of a lot of room – aka space. A tiny bathroom can seem larger than it is when it is stripped of clutter. Keep the surfaces clean and clutter free to give the buyer a feeling of more room to move around in.

When a buyer walks into your house and starts opening doors and pulling out drawers, you don't have to panic. With today's assignment completed, you can be proud of your perfectly presentable bathrooms. This was a hard day. Give yourself a break now and enjoy a nice hot shower. See you back here tomorrow.

# Day 9 – Grout That Goes Beyond Clean

The buyer needs to visualize themselves in your home. That's what we talked about from Day 1. Staging the rooms and furnishings is only one part of the picture. Another part of the picture is about the simple things that make people happy in their home.

Can a potential buyer see themselves walking around in bare feet after a nice bath?  Look down at the grout. Did the image just get a bit blurry? Your bathrooms got a good make-over yesterday, but now it's time to give them that one last touch.

## Your Mission

Grab those old toothbrushes you've been saving and get ready. Recruit the family, especially the ones with muscles and a good back. It's time to scrub, scrub, scrub. You can mix up a variety of pastes to find out what works best for you. One of my favorites is baking soda and hydrogen peroxide. Beware; it foams. But once it stops foaming you have an excellent scrub and disinfectant and for very little money. Other options are lemon juice, and baking soda and cider vinegar mixture.

Simply take the toothbrush, dip it in the paste, and spread the mixture on the grout in an area you can handle in one scrubbing. Let it sit for a few minutes, then scrub it into the grout with your toothbrush. Move to another area, then another, until all the grout is clean. Then, wash the tile and rinse it well.

It may be worth purchasing a grout sealer to apply once you have your grout perfectly clean. It will extend the job and prevent you from having to repeat this cleaning task too soon. There's no way around it; this is a difficult, time-consuming task. You don't want to do it more often than you must.

Now the grout is just as shiny clean as the rest of the bathroom. Your potential buyer can see their freshly bathed feet walking around on that floor. They can imagine their little toddler splashing around in that bathtub. They can imagine a steaming hot shower after a hard day. You've got your buyer's attention – in a good way!

# Day 10 – Clear Out the Garage and Basement

If you have been following the steps systematically, the interior of your house is now looking very nice. But as you prep your house for a sale, you have boxes piling up in the garage and/or the basement, or another storage area outside of the main living area of your house.

You might think that a garage packed full of stuff would give a buyer the idea that your garage holds a lot of stuff, right? Wrong. All that stuff works in just the opposite way. A garage or basement that is full of stuff indicates a LACK of storage space rather than plenty of space. When you show your buyer a large empty space, they see instantly that there is a lot of room for their stuff. Now that you've been decluttering the inside of the house and piling boxes up in your garage or basement, it's time to look at that space.

## Your Mission

Drive around any neighborhood and look at the houses with the garage doors open – Saturday and Sunday mornings are a good time to do this. Chances are you'll see more stuff than the owner will need in a lifetime. Basements offer the same sort of "out of sight, out of mind" storage space. When a buyer is looking for a new house, they want a garage or basement that doesn't resemble their own mess. When you stage your house for sale, you must consider your storage areas, too.

Start in the garage, carport, or other outdoors storage area that does storage duty. If you have sports equipment that's broken or out of season, pack it up or get rid of it. Be ruthless. Treat your garage like the last day of a clearance sale – everything must go!

Your garage should be as empty as possible. You aren't going to need most of that stuff in the next few months. Keep the good bikes, the tools you'll need for the current season, and paint cans for touch up. That's all you need. Again, be ruthless. If you have shelves, they should be only half full. This gives the impression of more space to fill. The buyer sees this space and thinks "Good. I have a place for my [whatever]." And that's exactly what you want them to think. You don't want a buyer to see your stuff filling the garage. You want the buyer to see *their* stuff filling the garage.

If you have a basement filled with goodies, you will need to clear that out, too. Some things are expected in storage areas, but again, a half-filled storage area looks larger than it is. A buyer can imagine their out-of-season clothes stored in the basement, but only if they're not looking

at your boxes of out-of-season clothes stuffed in corners and on shelves, or hanging on hooks everywhere. It's a funny concept, I know, but it's true. Your stuff in the basement makes the basement look crowded and small. A buyer can't imagine their stuff in there unless the area is mostly empty. If you don't want to pay for storage, have a garage sale!

Now that you've purged the unnecessary things from your garage and basement, it's time to deal with all those piles of boxes you hauled out of the house. No matter how neatly you pile them, the spacious feeling you worked so hard to achieve is gone. Remember, space equals value. It's time to rent a storage unit. The money you pay for a storage unit will come back to you quickly when you sell your house.

A potential buyer needs to envision their stuff in your house. They can't do that if they can't see the space available. Today is the day to clear out that garage and basement.

# Day 11 – Power Through the Exterior Grime

If it's a buyer's market you want your house to stand out from the crowd and if it's a seller's market you want to get the top price. There's no point in a quick sale if the price is less than it could be. Either way, if you want to properly prep your house for a sale, it will take more than sorting and organizing. It will take cleaning every inch of it. And, we're not talking about just the kitchen, bathroom, and bedrooms. No. Today, we're going outside.

Dead leaves, moldy exteriors, and grease spots on the driveway are all unappealing and can make your house undesirable. These things shouldn't turn buyers off, but they do. When buyers have lots of houses to look at, everything that makes your house stand out is a selling point. If your house is clean, really deep-down clean, sparkling clean, buyers will remember your house, which is what you want.

**Your Mission**

It's time to dig in and start getting the exterior of your home in order. This is not an easy process, so be sure to get help. This chore may even take you into tomorrow. So, let's get started.

You're going to start with one of the biggest jobs, which is also one of the most satisfying because results are immediately visible. Fire up the power washer. If you don't own one, you can rent one at your local hardware superstore or hire shop. Get your spouse or a friend to help you and work as a team. One of you can power wash while the other moves stuff out of the way. It can really get tiring, so take turns.

Start at the top. Clean out your gutters and power wash them. Move down the house, power washing under the eaves or anywhere that grime accumulates. Power wash the oil leaks and what-have-you off the driveway, the years of accumulated gunk off the driveway and the mildew off the walls. Power wash your back deck or patio, and your entry steps; you want everything perfect.

If you don't feel comfortable doing this task yourself, don't skip it. Hire a professional. The money spent will come back to you in a better sale. Be sure you check for proper insurance before beginning. Liability insurance for power washing is a specialized policy and can be very expensive. It is unlikely that the local handyman has the right coverage. Why is this important? If your professional power washer doesn't carry liability insurance, you may find yourself replacing your siding/cladding before you can sell.

This is a messy, time-consuming process, but one that will pay off. Things like blocked, messy gutters and black moldy siding/cladding happen to every homeowner, but from a buyer's point of view, those things just make them suspicious. Even though their home may have the same problems, when looking at a new home to buy, they can open up doubts and questions.

Plan this day well with a lot of time and a lot of help. When it's done, you'll have something to celebrate – a house that a buyer will remember, and for good reasons!

# Day 12 – The Windows Are The Jewel Of The House

We're still cleaning up outside today. The exterior of the house is difficult, so trying to do it in one day just won't work. Even though the work is tough, think of it as making money.

Now that all the heavy grime is removed, starting with the rain gutters and moving down the house and out to the street with the power washer, you are ready to shine things up. Be sure to double check that all those messy, grimy jobs have been done before you start the next step – washing the windows.

## Your Mission

Window-cleaning is not as hard as it looks, honest. But you need the right supplies. Be sure to get a good sturdy ladder and a couple of buckets that you can hang from the ladder. You'll need a nice big sponge, a squeegee, a little brush, and some rags in a plastic carry-all that you can attach to the ladder.

Choose your favorite cleaner and fill one bucket with cleaner and hot water. Fill the other bucket with clean cold water. Bring all your supplies up the ladder and dig in. Use the brush first to dislodge any dirt and grime from the corners, then scrub with the sponge, rinse, squeegee, and wipe any streaks with clean rags.

Move on to each window until you have them all shiny clean. Step back and admire your work. The windows really are the jewel of your home. If you have screens on the windows you might consider leaving them off at least the front windows. The reason is because the windows look nice and shiny without screens. The screens block the shine and dull the sparkle.

Window washing is hard work, so if you are not up to it, be sure to hire a professional window cleaner to get it done for you. This is not a job you want to skip. That all-important first impression makes a big difference when buyers are narrowing down their choices. You want your windows to sparkle, because that might just make a buyer's eyes sparkle, too!

# Day 13 – Wallpaper Has Been Hanging Around Too Long

Let me apologize in advance. Sorry. This task needs to be done. You need to remove the wallpaper. There are a few things that immediately age your house, and wallpaper is one of those things.

I know, I know. You spent hours agonizing until you choose just the perfect wallpaper or border. But, even if you had the hottest trend on your walls, trends change and buyers may not have the same tastes in design. Remember; you want a potential buyer to imagine their own things in your house and the only way they can do that is if the wallpaper is new or at the very least neutral. So, unless your wallpaper and borders are one of the above, they need to come down. Sorry.

## Your Mission

Buyers know that this task is a real pain, and something they absolutely do NOT want to tackle anytime soon. Unless you plan to sell your house at a fixer-upper price, you need to put in the work. Now, let's get real. This job may be tough, or it may not be that difficult. It all depends on the wallpaper and how it was applied. But, before you start scraping wallpaper, you have another task that will freshen and brighten your house just as much as removing the old wallpaper.

You will need to remove those other things that have been hanging around aging and darkening your house - the window coverings.

Drapes can make a room look dark and dated. You need to let light into your house. If taking all the drapes down doesn't make sense, then perhaps just lighten the look by removing valances or extra panels. Open your house to daylight as much as possible. If you need window coverings for privacy, keep them as simple as possible. If you already have blinds, but they are outdated, bent, torn, or just dirty, you need to spruce them up or replace them.

Now you can move on to the other thing that's been hanging around the house - the wallpaper.

Start by taking a wet sponge and soaking the wallpaper in an out of the way corner. Wait a minute or so, then carefully give it a tug. If it peels off easily, you are good to go. If it doesn't budge, soak it again, and try again. If it still doesn't budge, you will need some steaming equipment.

If it does peel off, you will probably notice a sticky or slimy substance on the back of the paper and the walls. This is the glue or paste that was used to hang the wallpaper. Even if the paper peels off easily with just water, you want to use a wallpaper paste remover meant to dissolve the glue so it comes off your walls. It's time now to head to your home improvement store.

Start by asking questions at the wallpaper section of the store. Use their expertise to direct you to the right tools of the trade. You may also want to Google any tips you can find to make the process smoother. Send the word out to family and friends to get any DIY tips they have to offer. This is one job that once you do it, you'll have a wealth of information to share. You may not get any recruits to help with the actual work, but you'll get a bunch of "been there, done that" advice. And that will save you a lot of time and frustration.

Let the experts steer you in the right direction. Don't skimp on the tools and products you'll find to physically steam, spritz, melt, and scrape the wallpaper off the walls. The proper tools, wallpaper paste remover, spritz bottle, wide scraper, and steamer, if necessary, are crucial to getting the job done right. Any job is easier with the right tools. Spend enough time and money so the wallpaper removal job doesn't overwhelm and disappoint you.

Once you have your tools and your tips, gather your reserve and dig in. Be sure to have a big garbage can ready for the wallpaper, as well as a big stack of rags. Cover the floor, especially up against the wall, with good absorbent rags. This process will produce a lot of water and slimy glue, so be prepared to clean up as you go.

With all your tools gathered, you can now begin. Depending on the amount of wallpaper you have, this could take all day, or even a couple days. This is a big job that produces a major improvement in your house's appeal. You will notice a lighter, brighter house when you're done.

We know that buyers like blank walls and bright, open windows. Give them what they want and they just might give you something you want – a sale!

# Day 14 – Be A Grime Fighter From Wall To Wall

Today, we're tackling something you knew was coming - washing the walls, base/skirting board molding, and other trim. If you removed wallpaper, you saw the mess around all the moldings. If you didn't get a chance to climb around on your hands and knees to remove wallpaper, you may want to do it now. You will be surprised how much grime you find when you take a closer look. Even in a very clean home, grime happens.

In this task, you'll remove any leftover paste from the now wallpaper-free walls, as well as spruce up dusty walls, greasy walls, and stubborn spills, smudges, and smears. No matter what you're faced with, a day spent cleaning up the biggest surfaces in your home – the walls – is well worth the effort.

## Your Mission

If you have removed wallpaper from your walls, you may want to start with a cleaning solution of fresh water and a little of the paste remover solution. Most of the slimy sticky glue should have been removed during the wallpaper removal process, but there could still be some residue. Take your time to wash off the glue. Once the glue is completely gone, let the walls dry, then follow up by wiping the walls down with clean water and rags. Now you can move onto your painted or wood paneled walls.

Even the cleanest looking walls can be covered with a layer of dust and pollen. This sort of dirt may not be obvious, but it can give an overall dull look to the walls. A simple dusting from top to bottom will knock down the loose stuff. A careful check of the corners, for cobwebs and dust bunnies, is very important.

As you're working your way down the walls, don't forget to wipe down the doors and the trim around the doors and windows. Once you've covered all the big surfaces, you'll want to remove smudges, fingerprints, and crayon graffiti with an appropriate cleaner.

And, now you have worked your way down from top to bottom. You are ready to attack those base/skirting boards. Why are these a separate item here? Somehow this molding becomes the catcher of juice, pet hair, food particles, hairspray, and plenty of unidentified globs. It is like a little magnet running the length of the room; and it's not just the kitchen, it's all through the house. So be prepared.

To clean around these boards, you're going to have to get on your knee pads and get down on the floor with your favorite cleaning product. Choose a good cleaner, simple soap and hot water or your favorite "green" product. Move from room to room and get those boards clean and glob free!

You really don't want a mystery substance stuck to a surface. I guarantee, if it's there, the buyer will see it. Be ready for their inspection so they will be ready with an offer!

## Day 15 – Treat The Walls & Ceiling To A Beauty Treatment

You've given your walls and woodwork a real heavy-duty scrubbing. You had to muscle your way through, which didn't leave you much time for detail. Today's the day to fine tune the little things you might have skipped. Your walls are clean, but it's time to take a closer look. This is like taking care of your skin after you exfoliate. Treat those little imperfections with tender care so your home's "skin" will look its best. Let's see what can be done to give your walls the spa treatment.

## Your Mission

Start by looking for any holes, small cracks, or tears in the wall surface that need to be filled. Now is not the time to try and hide imperfections like this. Now is the time to fix them. If you're just filling holes left from nails, for instance, you can often just fill the hole with a tiny bit of filling compound pushed into the hole with your finger. Anything bigger may need sanding and touch up with paint.

Even though cracks in drywall are normal as a house shifts and settles over the years, it still is disconcerting to a buyer. Cracks can be a real red flag to buyers. So, if you've been ignoring little cracks, fill them and touch them up with paint. If you're faced with big cracks, it's another thing entirely.

A big crack in a wall or the ceiling will scream "bad foundation" or "bad roof" or just plain "bad house." If the crack is too large for you to handle with confidence, call in a professional. Do not try to stuff a crack full of filling compound and pretend you never saw it. Buyers will notice and, if they don't, their inspector sure will. Call in a specialist and find out the truth. Then, have a professional fix it.

If the crayon and scuff marks didn't come off when you washed the walls, it is time to get tough with them. If you know that you are going to paint a particular room, just put a good primer on the mark and move on. If, however, a room's paint is fresh and neutral already, roll up your sleeves. Check all the latest information about how to remove stubborn stains from the walls and try them. There are erasers and solutions that are meant just for these kinds of jobs. If you absolutely can not remove the smudge, retouch with matching paint.

This is the type of chore that takes a real "buyer's eye." You may need someone else to walk through your house with a more critical approach. This is no time to be sensitive. All of us get accustomed to the little nicks and marks that we walk by every day. Be ruthless. If you have even one thought of "this is good enough" I can guarantee a potential buyer will be thinking just the opposite...

# Day 16 – Put Your Best Painted Face Forward

Wow! You are officially through the halfway mark. Great job! Isn't it good to know you are on the downhill slope from now on? You're getting closer and closer to the finish line. Take a deep breath and give yourself a pat on the back.

Right, that's enough. It's time to dig in again. There are two words about painting your walls that you must know – fresh and neutral. Fresh paint gives your walls a younger look. The other key word is "neutral." If your walls aren't a neutral color, potential buyers waste time trying to imagine them neutral. The more time they spend turning the walls neutral in their imagination, the more work they see. And that translates into more work for them, which may mean moving on to the next house. Even with the resurgence of color, if you're thinking of selling, you're better off with neutral. So, get out your paint supplies and accept the inevitable.

## Your Mission

You can't avoid it. Paint. I know you love that shade of orange. It's lovely. Personally, I have a penchant for lime green. But we must set our personal preferences aside. The truth is, buyers can get turned off by strong colors. It's quiz time now. Why are we stripping off all our personality from our house? Because potential buyers want to see themselves in the house – not you.

Even if you are a professional designer with a trendy bright red kitchen, a buyer doesn't want your design. Colors, any colors, prevent a buyer from visualizing themselves and their style in the house.

Remember, we are going for the quickest, most successful sale possible. Paint is a cheap way to make this happen. Start by choosing your paint colors, just so long as you choose paint with names that include gray, white, mushroom, cream, or neutral. That may sound like a bad joke, but when selling a house, it's the truth. When you go to the paint supply store, pull yourself away from that wall of rainbow and jewel colors. This is not your house anymore; it belongs to a buyer.

Choosing the finish for your paint may take some thought. Most formal rooms are perfectly fine with a flat paint. If you have uneven wall surfaces, flat paint will not emphasize imperfections like a glossy paint will. However, flat paint is not usually very washable and fingerprints and smudges can quickly detract from your fresh paint job.

For that reason, you may want to choose a satin or eggshell, which is a nice in-between option, especially if your house is being marketed as a family-friendly house. The kitchen and bathrooms are painted with a soft-sheen specialty paint because it is very washable and wears well. Trim around windows and doors is often painted in high-gloss although eggshell can also be used.

If you are painting over dark walls, you will probably need a primer. Put a little of your paint color into the primer to help the painting job go a little faster. The paint will cover better over the primer that has been tinted, usually resulting in having to use only two coats – the tinted primer, then the paint. If you are worried about paint fumes, are pregnant, or just don't want the smell of paint hanging around the house, you can buy low-odor paint. Be sure to question the person at the paint store to get all the information you need. That's what they are there for.

Preparation is 90% of the work when you paint, and since you already prepped the walls, the actual painting should go quickly. If painting seems like too much trouble, just remind yourself that painting is like money in your pocket - put there by a quick and successful sale.

# Day 17 – Freshen Up Floors To Finalize The Sale

Time to give those floors a once over. Not your regular quick mop, but with a concerted effort to bring your floors back to life. Without some special attention, floors quickly become tired and dull. They take a lot more wear and tear than probably any other area in your house.

In the regular course of your day, you probably don't see the floors all that much. If they're not covered in dirt, mud, and paw prints, you're happy. But now you have potential buyers who will notice every scratch and scuff. Let's get started removing those distractions.

**Your Mission**

Start with the scratches on the wood floors. Don't stress. You don't need to have them refinished, just spiffed up a bit. Usually the areas by the doors take the most abuse. A little elbow grease will bring them back to life. Scrub with a good scrub brush using a floor cleaner designed for the task. Rinse the floor well and buff it to dry.

For deeper scratches, use specialty wood fillers or markers to match the shade of your flooring, along with a high-end furniture polish. Patch and fill any scratches that need a little extra help. The furniture polish can then be rubbed in easily over the patched area with a soft cloth. For scratched areas that are less damaged but still noticeable, skip the filler and just rub in a generous amount of polish, then buff dry. Follow up by buffing the entire floor surface with thick cloth until the floors glow.

Ceramic tile floors need special attention, too. Start by repairing any broken tiles. They stick out like a sore thumb. Once that's done, you're

ready to begin. Clean all the grout thoroughly making sure you remove any stains.

When the grout is clean, get out your scrub brush and bucket. Again, a simple mopping won't do. Use a good cleaner and hot water, then rinse well. A little white vinegar in the rinse water will remove any soap residue. Then be sure to completely dry the floor with soft clean rags to keep the floor from having water spots.

Linoleum and vinyl flooring have their own special care. Begin with repairs. These kinds of flooring can come loose after years of wear and tear, especially along the seams. Re-glue, re-stick, or otherwise reattach the offending section. If the floor is truly awful, it may be worth the expense to replace it. Even a less expensive flooring like the peel-and-stick style look better than a torn, stained, faded, or outdated floor.

When you are satisfied with the condition of your linoleum or vinyl flooring, it's time to give it a good shine. Again, put away your damp mop and get out your scrub brush. Use a good cleaner, then follow up with a good rinse. Dry with a clean rag. Some older linoleum will benefit from waxing. Other flooring has built in wax and adding more on top won't do it any good. In this case, just focus on getting the floor clean and buffing it dry until it shines.

A potential buyer has a lot to look at when they walk in your door. Make sure the first thing they notice isn't a big stain, scratch, or tear in the flooring. And just in case you're thinking about putting a rug down to hide a bad area, think again. Buyers will pull up rugs and uncover your ugly secret, and there goes your top price, if not your sale.

# Day 18 – Buyers Give Kudos To Clean Carpets

Now that your wood, tile, and vinyl floors are in mint condition, let's give those carpets and area rugs the full treatment. Yes, a quick vacuum is usually not enough to restore carpeting and large rugs to their original luster.

Take a good, hard look at the fabrics on your floor. If your eye immediately goes to the spots and worn traffic paths, so will your potential buyer's eye. When this happens, the buyer automatically starts calculating; replace carpet equals money. That's less money offered meaning less money on your side of the closing statement. It could even squelch the sale completely. Let's look at this common complaint and what you can do to help eliminate the problem and make the sale.

Have the carpets steam-cleaned. There are three ways to go about this; professional, rent a machine or buy a machine. Your decision will depend on your abilities, the amount of carpet to clean, and your budget.

To me, the first and best option is to hire a professional. Hunt down one of those offers for multi-room, one-price discounts. Choose a few and give them a call. I have found great cleaning companies offering an inexpensive service for three rooms and not so great cleaning companies charging exorbitant fees. So, be choosey. There are also different methods to consider carefully. Dry chemical cleaners may or may not work for you. Ask around, shop around, and choose the best cleaning deal that you can live with.

Your next option is to rent one of those heavy-duty steam cleaners. This is a good alternative to 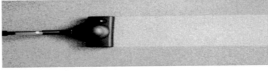 professional cleaning, but only if you can do the work. This type of carpet cleaning works well also if your carpet area is smaller. If you have, or can get, the muscle to pick up this machine, use it (don't forget the stairs), and then take it back, you may want to consider this type of carpet cleaning (it is heavy!). There is a convenience factor here; clean when you want, where you want, with less whole house disruption. But, again, you must be prepared to do the work. Are they as thorough as a professional carpet steam cleaning? Maybe not. You would have to make that judgment.

The final option is to buy a steam cleaning machine. There is a variety on the market now in many price ranges. If you have small areas of carpeting, this may be an option. They work well for spots and stains, as well as cleaning traffic areas. This option is a lot slower because you'll be cleaning smaller areas at a time. One advantage, of course, is that you can use your machine whenever you want. This is especially handy throughout the time when you are showing your house. If you see an area start to look less than clean, or you spill something, you can clean it up right away. The convenience factor is something to consider. But, to clean a house full of carpeting?  This would have to be part of your decision-making process.

If your carpeting has lost its youthful appeal, you may want to have it professionally re-stretched, sort of like a face lift. Covering up ripples in the carpet with area rugs is a definite no-no. A buyer will quickly discover the wrinkles and will just as quickly calculate the price of repair... or they may just move on. Better to fix or tear out the carpeting than losing the sale.

Area rugs and room size carpeting are just fine if they are an asset to the room, and not just there to cover up a bad floor. Make sure both are in good repair. If you have a piece of carpet down with raw edges, get rid of it. Or, if it's a valuable piece that enhances the décor of the room, get the edges stitched professionally.

The fabric you have on the floor takes a beating. Between outside elements coming in on your shoes, kids and fizzy drinks, pets doing what pets sometimes do, those carpets take a real beating. Money spent cleaning and freshening your carpets and rugs will pay off. You don't want to see your buyer move on to the next house when something as simple as a clean carpet could have kept them interested.

# Day 19 – The Ins And Outs Of Doors And Windows

Today we are going to open some doors for you. Not figuratively, but literally. Then we're going to throw open some windows, too. Why all the commotion?  You need to inspect your doors and windows for all those little (or big) things that could irritate or frustrate a potential buyer as they move through your house.

Your inspection will include more than the cleanliness and sparkle. You will need to stop, look, and listen to every door and window. This chore also takes more than a few cleansers and rags. Let's take a walk through with a critical eye, and ear, to get these elements of your house in order.

## Your Mission

Get on your tool-belt. No, I'm not kidding. This task will involve at least one screwdriver, a hammer, and some sort of oil or silicone. You will want to have rags along, also. As you move through the house, opening and closing doors and windows, you will be looking and listening for problems.

Start with the doors, exterior, and interior. Make sure they all open and close properly. If it squeaks, add some silicone spray or WD-40 to the hinges. If the door knobs look or function less than perfect, fix them or replace them. For exterior doors, you'll want to check the weather stripping for a good, clean seal.

Throw open the windows. If you rarely open your windows, you may not even be aware of problems. But, a potential buyer will unlock those windows and open them, or try to. They will pull back the curtains, pull up the blinds, and take a good look. Can you afford to make a mistake by having a window that is less than perfect? Or even painted shut!

Check every window to see if they open and close. Do they lock? Are there any broken panes? If so, get them fixed. How are the screens? Where are the screens?  Is there any paint on the glass?  Are there big problems, such as a broken seal (that's the hazy look that a window gets when the insulated seal is broken)? You will either need to have the window replaced or you will be giving the buyer credit to do so.

Do not try to hide problems. Buyers will notice and will not be happy. Right or wrong, a buyer may automatically assume that if one window is bad, all the windows are bad, and they will deduct a figure immediately from the price of your house. If doors are sticking and squeaking, and if windows are painted shut, your house just screams "fix me!" And when buyers hear that, they plug their ears and walk away.

With a few tools in your belt and a critical look at the doors and windows, you can spruce up your house in a big way. Don't give potential buyers reasons to look the other way. Give them reasons to envision themselves in this perfectly fine-tuned house!

# Day 20 – Tame The Mechanical Monsters

This is the day you've been dreading. You will be tackling the dreaded mechanical systems. That would be your heating and cooling systems, water system, electrical system, and anything else that helps your house function as a home.

Next to a private water well or tank, and the roof, buyers worry about the mechanical systems the most. And with good reason. A mechanical problem is an expensive surprise, and buyers do not like surprises. It's time to dig in and learn everything you can about the internal workings of your house.

## Your Mission

Start with a call to your heating and cooling people. Get an inspection and tune-up on the boiler, air conditioner, and related equipment. If that requires a thorough cleaning, do that, too. If the professionals find a problem, get an estimate for repairs. If the equipment checks out, ask for a certificate to attach to your home sale paperwork.

Your job now is to keep up with the maintenance. If you only change the boiler filter or filters when a buyer is coming to look, you are only doing your boiler, and you, harm. If you allow leaves to pile up around an outside air conditioning unit, all your hard work, and money, will be wasted. So, get your heating and cooling system in perfect working order and keep it that way.

Move on to your water heater and other water-related equipment, such as pumps. Again, put a call into a professional. Getting a plumber to inspect, clean, and certify the water equipment goes a long way to putting a buyer's mind at rest. If you have water softening equipment, make sure you get that checked as well.

One area some sellers forget is the electrical system. However, a look inside your circuit breaker box will tell you why this is also an important step. It's complicated and scary! Call in an electrician to give you, and your buyer, peace of mind. Are all the circuit breakers at the proper amperage? The job of the circuit breaker is to "trip" if the load is too much for the line. Make sure every circuit breaker is properly rated and installed. If you have an older home with a fuse box, be sure that you have new fuses and, again, at proper amperage.

Also, even though this is not necessarily a function issue, buyers can get very suspicious of a confusing, messy, circuit breaker box. The area around and inside your circuit breaker box should be clean and well lit. An added extra is to clearly label a list of the circuits inside the box and what is on which circuit. Those little things mean a lot.

What else?  Don't overlook things like clothes dryer vents, gas stove vents, pool filters and pumps, sump pumps, water filtration systems, humidifiers, dehumidifiers, built in grills, gas fireplaces, wood fireplaces, automatic lights, etc. etc. Phew!

Think about everything that operates in your house to your life easier. Make sure it's working at peak performance. Also, make sure it looks good, is clean, and has nothing to make the buyer stand back and wonder if it really works. Remember, perception is still part of the sale. Make your house work for you to help clinch the sale.

**Day 21 – Keep The Conversation Going With Reliable Repair Estimates**

Today, we need to address the big-ticket items in your house. Before you start seeing yourself with an empty wallet, we're not saying you must fix all the things that need fixing. What you do need to do is be prepared. That means getting estimates for the major repairs.

For instance, if you are not able to replace that orange toilet and sink, replace the windows that need replacing, or update the boiler, you need to get an up-to-date estimate for what those repairs would cost. Potential buyers will appreciate the information and you will be ready to talk money when the time comes. Let's take a look at how this might work.

## Your Mission

The best way to approach an issue with your house is head-on. Your agent can include a conversation about any flaws with your house when he or she is showing the house, but already having an estimate for repairs opens the conversation rather than closing it. Leaving repair costs up to the imagination of the buyer is never a good idea. If you give them actual figures, they know immediately how they can proceed. The buyer will take those repairs into consideration when making their offer, eliminating wasted time and frustration.

Obviously, making repairs before you put your house on the market will help eliminate those obstacles to a sale. However, sometimes it just can't be done. By getting reliable estimates to repair problems, you can at least make the topic as painless as possible.

That will keep the conversation going, maybe all the way to a quick sale.

## Day 22 – Fix Simple Problems Outside To Draw Buyers Inside

It's another day to don your work belt and get back outside for more repairs. Like every other job we're attacking, we're eliminating all doubt for the buyers by getting as close to perfection as possible.

Most homeowners can do these jobs or a least some of them. However, if you feel less than capable, hire a handy person. You just need to have someone who can swing a hammer, climb up and down a ladder, mix a little quick-drying concrete, use sandpaper, handle a screwdriver, and ascertain if anything further needs to be done.

Again, you'll need a critical eye, so if you're blind to the faults of the house, get someone else. There is no room for "But, it's always been this way." Time to look at all those things you have not wanted to look at.

### Your Mission

Begin by making a list. Take a walk around the outside of your house, and carry a notepad. You'll want to make a quick note of every area that needs attention. To get you started on the right track, here's a quick checklist that can help. Follow along and check to make sure all the following are tight, affixed properly, not broken, not cracked, clean and in general working condition:

Shingles (any loose or missing?)
Foundation (any cracks?)
Doorbell (does it ring? Buyers check!)
Fence (all nails and boards present and accounted for?)
Mailbox (in good repair?)
Walkway (any cracks or tripping hazards?)
Deck (any loose boards? Still nice and clean from that power washing?)
Yard (edged and freshly mowed?)
Shutters (any loose or missing?)

What do you need to know once the inventory is done? It's simple.

If it's loose, tighten it.
If it's jammed, loosen it.
If it's broken, fix it.
If it's dirty, clean it.
If it's missing, find it.
If it's disappeared, replace it.

You get the picture. Aim for being the best house on the street. Don't give the buyers even one reason to walk away.

A buyer may not look twice at the fact that you have an extra linen closet, but they will notice the missing wood slats on the fence. Yes, buyers are that fickle. Know and accept what the buyer wants. Now is not the time to get stubborn. Give in and give 'em what they want!

# Day 23 – Buyers Bug Out When Pests Are Present

You know where they are. You've been exasperated and grossed out by them for some time. Bugs, or creepy crawlies if you prefer. If you know you have bugs, any kind of bugs, you need to deal with the problem aggressively, right now. Spraying some Raid around before a viewing will not give you the solution you need.

Hornets, wasps, ants, spiders, cockroaches, ladybugs, mosquitoes, and termites all must be dealt with. Some you can tackle by yourself with the help of the right equipment. For others, you will need to call in the professionals. Let's look at some general ideas to get a handle on these pests.

## Your Mission

Of course, you need to eliminate things that attract the bugs in the first place. Keep food in airtight containers. Back when you were cleaning the pantry you should have picked boxed or bagged food off the floor and moved food out of lower shelves. Depending on where you live, you may have to refrigerate even dry food items or at least put them in glass jars with tight lids.

Now that you've removed some of the typical bug-attracting sources, simple things can stop the most common bugs in their tracks. Place roach traps behind cabinets and appliances, but make sure they are completely out of sight. Use specific products on ant hills to stop the progression of ants into your house.

There's not a lot you can do for spiders, except make sure you routinely knock down their webs when you see even the smallest one appear. You'll find sprays that target wasps and hornets' nests. As soon as you spot a tiny nest, attack it with the proper spray immediately, following instructions very carefully.

There's also some to attack bees' nests but destroying those is not the best thing for the environment so a beekeeper is the best option. They will usually come free of charge to remove them.

If you live in a wooded or swampy area, you're going to have to keep on top of these creepy crawlies. It may be more economical, and more efficient, to hire a professional service to do the job. Consider "greener" alternatives if all those chemicals concern you. Many professionals are offering all sorts of packages for termination of those bug problems.

Even though termites are the obvious deal-breaker in countries concerned, many times the buyer decides to walk away when any kind of bugs are brought to their attention. Avoid this disappointment by dealing with bugs today. Don't make your buyers rush out the door on their way out to another house when they see bugs scurrying across the floor. Do what you must do, to remove those pests and bring in the buyers!

# Day 24 – Tackle Small Irritations Around The House

Today, let's slow the pace and work on some miscellaneous jobs. You've been working hard to get your house ready for sale. Some of the work has been back-breaking. The chores you'll be tackling today are the kind of things that you can do without muscle and brawn.

The bigger jobs around the house are definitely important. But, those little irritations that you don't notice anymore can also be important. It's the overall look and feel that will keep the buyer from leaving quickly. Let's take a walk through those little tasks and take care of them now.

**Your Mission**

Grab a notepad and go from room to room, taking a close look at every nook and cranny. Make notes about anything that doesn't look like a "model home." For instance, as silly as it seems, you want the plates on the light switches and outlets to not only be in good order but to match. An old brass plate sticks out like a sore thumb among all white plastic

covers. It's not a big thing, but it is something that distracts a buyer from imagining themselves in your house. Start your hardware store shopping list.

Another "big/little" irritation to buyers is a burned out light bulb. Imagine a buyer taking the time to go through your house, only to flip a switch and, nothing. The buyer came to see the room and if it's in the dark, how will they see it? What do they do? Come back another time after you've replaced the bulb? Wait while you or your realtor scramble around looking for a light bulb? Get out a flashlight? None of those options are going to make your potential buyer happy. Make sure you have a good supply so any time a light bulb burns out, you've got one to replace it right away. Again, don't give your buyer a reason to raise an eyebrow. Add light bulbs to your shopping list.

Now it's time to grab a screwdriver or two and investigate all those drawer pulls, cabinet knobs, and hinges. Your doors and drawers are going to take a beating while buyers walk through, opening, closing, opening, closing, and on and on, everything that moves. It's better to check each piece of hardware than to wait for one to fall off in a buyer's hand. Cabinet doors that are swinging by one hinge are not only an eyesore, they are dangerous. Check and tighten anything that's loose. If you notice anything missing, or mismatched, add it to your shopping list. You don't have to spend a lot of money on new hardware, just make sure the hardware you have matches and works.

Other little jobs that you may need to tackle are things like too many electrical cords tangled up and exposed. Neaten them up using boxes or tubes or whatever you can find to corral those cords. If you have electrical cords stuck under rugs, remove them and figure out a way to eliminate those highways of cords. And, if you have added multiple plug-in extensions to any electrical outlets, unplug them. If you have a double outlet, you can have two things plugged in. Anything more than that looks dangerous and alerts the buyer to the possibility that you don't have enough outlets in your house. This distracts buyers from what they should be doing – imagining their furnishings in your house.

Switch covers, outlet covers, hinges, knobs, and electrical cords. How can any of that really matter?  By simply taking the buyer's eye away from your house's good points, the focus can change rapidly; and not to your advantage. Your floors are shiny, your carpets are clean, your windows shine, and your walls are spotless. That's what you want your buyers to see. Don't distract them with minor irritations. You want a potential buyer to keep their 'eye on the prize' – your house!

## Day 25 – Out With Obnoxious Odors

This topic might be a little sensitive, but it's best to face it head on. You need to do a smell test. Houses can have a smell to them that the occupants do not even notice. It could be a cat litter odor or a cooking odor. Maybe you have a musty basement or a carpet that smells stale. Odors like cigarette smoke, wet dogs, and hamsters are part of life. But when you're selling your house, you have to be especially aware of what other people are smelling.

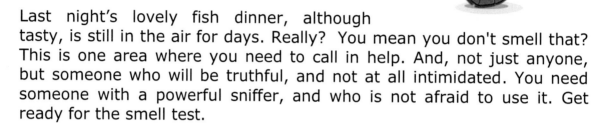

Last night's lovely fish dinner, although tasty, is still in the air for days. Really? You mean you don't smell that? This is one area where you need to call in help. And, not just anyone, but someone who will be truthful, and not at all intimidated. You need someone with a powerful sniffer, and who is not afraid to use it. Get ready for the smell test.

**Your Mission**

When you find someone with your best interests at heart, ask them to walk into your house and give you their first impression. This is not a visual test. You may even suggest they close their eyes when they walk in the front door and just rely on their sense of smell. The person you ask to perform this task must be brutally honest with you. Once your chosen 'sniffer' has identified the odors, you'll need to track them down. The easiest way to get rid of odors is to hunt them down at their source.

Pet odors may be the easiest to identify and find, but the hardest to get rid of. Snowball and Rover may not be able to live at Grandma's while you stage your house for sale, so you're going to need to find another solution. Be fastidious with that cat litter box, cleaning it out daily and washing it every week. Dog beds and dog houses need to be scrubbed and freshened and moved to a vented area. You may even need to make sure Rover gets the spa treatment at the groomers much more often. *Baking soda and cider vinegar added to washing water work wonders for pet odor.*

Food odor is another obvious offender. Cooking creates wonderful aromas, but only when you're sitting down to the meal. The lingering odors of onion, garlic, fish, and other pungent smells hang on drapes, rugs, and in the air. One solution is to use a good vent hood while you're cooking. If you don't have a range hood with a vent, it may be wise to install one. If you do and you're not using it, start. And if you have a range hood with a filter instead of an outside vent, wash it. You may also want to consider moving your cooking outside when possible. If you know you're going to be showing your house, don't fry fish inside the night before. Sometimes common sense is the best defense against odor.

The bathroom can harbor mold and mildew which can be detected by a sensitive sniffer. Be sure always to use your bathroom fan whenever you are in the bathroom. Keep the toilet spotless and the drains clean. Each drain, by design, has standing water in it. Keep that water fresh and clean. A small amount of bleach poured into the drain daily will help keep the drain clean. If you don't like using bleach, a little lemon juice or vinegar works well, also.

If there is a smoker in the house, it's time to move them outside. The smell of smoke can be a real deal-breaker for some people. They may be allergic, or they may just suspect that with the first whiff of smoke, they'll have to tear out all the carpeting and scrub down all the walls and the ceiling to get rid of it. You may have already done all that, but if the smell is there, your potential buyer will be suspect.

When you're trying to rid your house of any lingering odors, you must be ruthless. And, please please please... this is not the time to plug in some air freshener gadgets. The smell is unmistakable and says that you are trying to cover something up. Get rid of the odors at their source and stay on top of it daily. When your house is fresh smelling as well as neat and cozy, potential buyers will easily be able to imagine themselves settling right in.

# Day 26 – The Dining Room Is The Room Of Dreams

I know you have too much furniture in your dining room. How do I know? Because most people do. Remember our lessons from day one? An empty space makes a appear bigger. You would think just the opposite. Shouldn't a buyer see a table that seats eight and think "Wow! This room is big enough for a table that seats eight." Instead, the room looks crowded, which makes it appear smaller than it is.

We're going to give the buyer what they want – openness and spaciousness. You want them to imagine their own dining room set filling that space. Maybe they can even imagine a new, bigger set, but not if you've already filled it up. That visual has the buyer limiting their imagination. The buyer is now thinking; "Squished, crowded, my family will never fit. This dining room won't work. This house won't work." Time to do something about your dining room.

## Your Mission

It's time to get over the idea that your dining room table that seats eight should have eight chairs around it. You may want to remove the leaf, if you have one in place, and make the table smaller. A smaller table with only four or six chairs leaves space for the eye to wander, and imagine the possibilities.

If you have a big table without a leaf, just reducing the chairs will make a difference. You can take a couple chairs out and set them on either side of the buffet, or remove them altogether. Remove the chairs from both heads of the table, especially if the chairs have arms. This will allow much more room around the table and will have the buyer thinking; "Wow! This space is HUGE. Imagine how many people I could get in here over the holidays. I might even have space for my Grandmother's sideboard."

And, speaking of sideboards, if your buffet or sideboard is dominating the room, remove it. If that's not possible, try rearranging the room to get the buffet out of the traffic pattern. Give it some thought, draw it out on graph paper, then experiment with room design. The dining room is often crowded because the furniture is so big. You need to work around this by re-thinking the way the room is set up.

Dinnerware and accessories are also space-absorbing items. Clean out everything that doesn't fit in a particular spot in the buffet. Keep the table clear of clutter and limit the accessories on the table and buffet to a few coordinating pieces. Choose a mirror and a few prints to hang on the wall. Keep the dining room as minimalist as possible so the buyer can imagine filling it up with their stuff.

Draperies or other window treatments should be kept to a minimal amount. A lot of heavy fabrics will give the appearance of a crowded room. Draperies that darken the room also give the buyer the feeling that the room is small and crowded. Let in the light and reduce the amount of fabric around the windows to lighten the dining room. If you have blinds, make sure they are drawn up to let the light in.

Although a dining room may be a luxury item for some home buyers,  when a buyer sees a dining room, they typically fall in love with the idea. Thoughts of big dinners with family and friends take over, and the more they can imagine themselves in your dining room, the more likely they are to keep looking. This is the room that shiny magazines love to feature at holidays. This is the room that buyers can call home – but only if you stage it for them!

# Day 27 – Say Good Bye To Your Personality

Take a minute right now to pat yourself on the back. Getting your house staged perfectly for a quick sale is by no means easy. I never said it would be, but I just want to acknowledge that you are right; this job is really, really tough. The work is hard physically, as well as being emotionally draining at times, but you've accepted and excelled at the challenge and have come through like a champ. Kudos to you.

For today, let's slow the pace a bit. It's time to sit for a minute, relax, and take a deep breath because this is the day you may have been dreading the most. Today you will need to say goodbye to your house, your home, and all the memories it holds for you. Walk around and let go. Breathe in. Breathe out. Begin.

## Your Mission

As you walk around the house, you'll need to collect any little personal items you missed during the first de-cluttering assignments. Those family photos, diplomas, trophies, and artwork by the kids all need to come down and be packed away carefully. Don't worry. You'll be bringing them out again soon. That's what staging your house for a quick sale is all about. Getting out of your old house and into your new home quickly. The faster you do this, the sooner you can bring your pictures and personal items back out.

I know it's difficult, but you need to be ruthless with your personal items. The wall space should be free of family pictures. It may seem silly but walls that are bare, except for a mirror or two or a large painting over the sofa, draw in potential buyers to the space.

If you have bookcases, however, they may benefit from a few small, nicely framed family pictures if they are arranged artfully. Now, there are differing camps on this. The first group feels that a few strategically placed photos can create a warm, fuzzy feeling in your house; a this-is-a-home feeling. The other side feels that a family photo prevents potential buyers from visualizing your house as their home. You'll need to make your own decision on that. But everyone agrees; a wall full or bookcase full of family photos is a no-no.

And, speaking of bookcases, take another look at the items you have left after you de-cluttered earlier. Are those little figurines you love still all lined up?  Is there a forgotten bowl of candy, old cut flowers, or a houseplant that needs attention?  Is there a basket of dog toys, cat toys, or even kids' toys?  These are all personal items, too, that need to be removed or at least put in attractive closed containers. Again, the idea is to give the potential buyer a clean space to imagine their personal items taking up residence. If your 'family' is already there, it's harder to imagine.

Don't give a buyer any reason to walk away. Your potential buyer may be able to see through the clutter and imagine the possibilities, or maybe they can't. Do you want to take the chance? No. Make sure your house is not interfering with a potential buyer's vision of their family's own pictures on the wall or their own special collections in the bookcases.

Harden your resolve and pack away those precious personal things. It won't be long before you'll be able to put everything back in a place of honor again. It's all for a good cause - staging your house for a quick sale so you can move on.

# Day 28 – Help Buyers See Beyond The Junk Room

Remember the 'junk room' you cleared out at the beginning of this project? Now that it's an empty space, a potential buyer can see the possibilities. But, you can do more to spark a buyer's imagination with this room.

Today we're going to add extra value to your house by showing buyers exactly what they're getting. This is where you are going to turn that junk room, or spare room, into the bonus room buyers are looking for. Rather than trusting your buyer to see the room as an asset, provide a possible use for that space. You're going to show the buyer the potential by staging that spare room.

## Your Mission

What you want to do is find a solution to a limitation your house may have. For instance, if your house only has a few bedrooms, you may want to stage this room as another bedroom or as a guest space. If your house is perfect for a professional working family, provide an office space. Set up a nice desk with an office chair and maybe a comfy chair in the corner with an end table and reading light. It doesn't take much, just a quiet cozy place that looks inviting and organized.

If your house and neighborhood are all about families, perhaps your spare room would be the perfect play room. Set up a small stage, hang a curtain, and add a bin of dress up clothes. Set up a table with the toy trains and trucks. Put dolls in a toy crib. Hang a chalkboard, shelves, and anything to help keep the space organized but fun at the same time. Don't let this room get cluttered! You want it to be a place to play, but the same rules apply in this room as the rest of the house; give the buyer an opportunity to visualize their own family in the house.

Remember, you don't want anything to look cluttered, nor do you want this newly appointed 'spare room' to feature your personal life. Even if the room is set up as an office, make it generic with all your personal items removed. If it's a play room, keep a wide variety of toys set up, but nothing personalized. If you're setting up a craft room or sewing room, keep it clean and, again, generic. A few bolts of fabric, an array of

ribbons, and some spools of thread are fine if it's all arranged neatly. A pretty container to hold scissors, stamps, punches, marking pens and other craft items is fine, too.

Another trick to help clean the clutter while you clear the buyer's mind is to use solid color bins to hold the clutter. That way you can mask what's inside so your potential buyer can use their own imagination about what the room can be used for. Those bins may hold scrapbooking supplies, sewing notions, office supplies, or coloring books. Let your buyer decide what this neat-as-a-pin extra room could become for their family.

When you emptied out your 'junk room' you created a clean slate for your potential buyers to imagine what they would put in this bonus space. Now you have given them a few suggestions. Think of this spare room as a fancy restaurant menu. When the wait-person walks up to your table and starts reading off the menu, your mouth starts watering. You thought you would order a steak, but now that you're listening to a description of Boeuf Bourguignon, you're all in!

To me, this is one of the most fun rooms to stage because you can use your imagination and play around with lots of options. If you don't absolutely need to use this room, stage it in a fun, creative way that you might not do in the rest of the house. You are almost done, but not quite. See you tomorrow when it's time to bring out the inner Inn Keeper in you!

## Day 29 – Play Host Instead Of Seller

You're in the final stretch. You can see the finish line. Today is a fun day, but you're not quite ready to sit back and relax. But, that's alright because I think you'll enjoy today's assignment – playing Bed and Breakfast hosts.

Picture yourself walking into a Bed and Breakfast, a fancy Inn, or a nice cozy hotel. What do YOU notice when you stay in one of these places? Is it the aroma?  Perhaps it's the fresh flowers everywhere. Or is the clean fluffy rugs and the crisp, bright white pillow cases?  Give it some thought, and then let's get going.

### Your Mission

It's time to add all the last little touches that most people forget when they get their home ready for sale. A professional house stager knows about the things that bring a buyer back. These aren't the things like square footage, number of closets, or size of the garage. It's not even about the age of the roof or windows. What the stager knows is that a buyer gets a 'feeling' about a house first. They may not even notice the individual touches, but the buyer recognizes the feeling of home.

Aroma is a big part of creating a feeling of home. The sense of smell is a powerful tool, either positive or negative. The plain fact is, when we smell something, it either makes us feel good or it makes us feel not so good. We can't know what each buyer will like aroma-wise, but there are some widely accepted aromas that just say HOME. The smell of cinnamon rolls is one such aroma. Or, if that doesn't work for you, there are many excellent candles that mimic the aroma quite well. Cookies are another nice aroma that helps set a homey stage. With those two aromas hovering around the kitchen and dining room, your potential buyer not only sees your clean house but feels your warm home.

The bathrooms and utility room need a fresh aroma. The easiest way to achieve this is, once you get them clean, is to add citrus products. For whatever reason, the smell of citrus, such as lemon, grapefruit, or orange, says "clean and fresh."  You might think, because they are fruit, that the brain would think "food" but it just doesn't work that way. You can make your own potpourri out of the peelings of citrus or you can use citrus oils or candles. Citrus scented cleaners are another way to keep the fresh smell going.

Bedrooms need a fresh smell, as well as a soothing smell. A teeny tiny bit of floral aroma goes a long, long way. You don't want anything too sweet or too strong. Some people like the smell of lavender, and some people don't. Keep small sachets of a blend of sweet herbs and fresh florals in the bedroom. You can also buy sprays, sachets, and candles that have a 'fresh linen' aroma. Try those out. Have a trusted friend give you their opinion about the aroma in your bedroom. You need a 'new nose' to tell you if you've gone overboard. Then, take their advice and adjust your aromas.

Aside from aroma, there are several items that turn a house into a home. You'll know them when you see them. Here's a reminder.

You want fresh, clean, and crisp sheets, pillowcases, and bedding on all the beds. If you can't afford full sets of sheets, at least get new pillowcases and a new duvet cover or coverlet so the whole bed at least looks new. Picture the bed in the fanciest hotel you've been in and try to emulate that the best you can. Remember; the buyer isn't going to be crawling into your bed, so in this case, a surface spruce-up is just fine.

Don't forget the little touches on the end tables and dressers. A small fresh flower arrangement is perfect in the master bedroom. New candles on the dresser and a beautiful fluffy rug say "cozy." For the kids' rooms, you don't need anything fancy; just nicely made beds and a big rug. Keep it simple so you can keep it clean and neat.

It's time to hang those new towels in the bathrooms. These are the ones that the family knows are not for their use!  Keep the family's towels under the sink or in the cupboard. Your pretty towels don't have to be expensive. They just have to be new, fresh, clean, and preferably in a complimentary color that goes with the neutral paint in the bathroom.

In the living areas, you want new candles, fresh flowers, and lots of fluffed up pillows on your sofa and chairs. You don't want to get too fussy because you could start to sneak back into the cluttered look if you're not careful. Throw pillows and nicely folded afghans are perfectly acceptable and turn your clean-living room into a cozy living room.

Another layer in your house that we discussed before deserves another mention. Light. When you walk into a beautiful Bed and Breakfast, you may notice the light before you notice anything else. Softly streaming light over a shiny wood floor just says; "Welcome!"  Be sure you have taken every advantage of all the natural light. If you have a dreary weather day for your showing, turn on lamps and light candles. A cozy house on a rainy day is also appealing as long as light warms the mood.

You want to "cozy up" your outside areas, also. Place a few potted plants artfully around the entrance. Choose flowering plants that suit the season. And, as common as this seems, you need a "Welcome" mat. No, it doesn't have to say "Welcome" but you do need a real mud-collecting mat at the entrance. This serves two purposes: it says "this is a home", and it catches the mud and dirt being tracked in by your buyers. You can't exactly tell a potential buyer to wipe their feet, but a good outdoor mat will catch a lot of the crud and grime.

Now turn around and walk into your house. What's the first thing you notice? Does it smell nice? Is it light and airy? Now walk down the hall into the bathrooms and bedrooms. Do the beds look fresh? Is there any reason why a buyer would want to quit looking at this point? Describe the aroma. Now move into the living room. Do you see a sofa and a few chairs or do you see an invitation to curl up with a good book?

The people in charge of staging those fancy lodgings, like your favorite Bed and Breakfast, country Inn, or hotel, know something about drawing people in and keeping them coming back. And, isn't that exactly what you want to do with a potential buyer? When you get a buyer to walk in the door, give them a reason to come back... with an offer!

Tomorrow is the final day. It's a big day to celebrate, but it's also a day to learn. I'll meet you right back here to wrap up this incredible journey.

Congratulations! You've made it to the final day on this month-long journey. Your house looks neat, clean, well-maintained, impeccable, flawless, loved, warm, and inviting. There is no way around it; this was not an easy task. It took a lot of work. You had many times when you were ready to throw in the towel and just settle for less. But you knew that meant less money, and that was not okay.

So, the hard work is over, right? Not exactly. This day's mission will actually take more than a day. Don't be misled. The assignment is a simple one, but one that many sellers find a bit difficult.

## Your Mission

You have only three things left to do...

1. Maintain
2. Maintain
3. Maintain

Sounds like this could be the easiest part of this entire process in getting your house ready and staged for sale. However, this is often the part that drives sellers crazy. Why? Because you are still living in the house. And your family is still doing, well, family things. Those things cause messes. There is only one way to handle this situation. Your perfectly staged house takes maintenance.

You will need to live in your house pretending that someone is coming to look at it in five minutes. Every day, every minute, you are on task. And, not just you, but your whole family. Everyone must get on board with this task.

The rules are: No matter how tired you are, no matter how late you work, no matter how crazy the kids are, the house MUST remain perfectly staged. That means that nothing gets out of place, messed up, or cluttered.

Mom, Dad, kids, pets, everybody has to stay on track. That means hang up clothes, use only the 'family' towels, wipe feet, do dishes, put away movies and music, and put the remote controls away. Nothing, absolutely nothing, can be dropped anywhere. School bags, mail, coats, hats, and boots go where they belong.

Use a few simple strategies to stay ahead of a full-out cleaning job. Keep paper towels handy so each family member can wipe down the sinks when they use them. Invest in a dusting mop to pick up dust and hair on the floors every day. On Day 29 your house looked like a model home. You need to keep it looking exactly like that.

I can almost guarantee you that buyers will want to come and see your house at the most inopportune times. It's the "Murphy's Law" of selling a house. So make sure the towels are straightened, the pillows are fluffed up, and everything is shiny clean and clutter free. ALL THE TIME.

Sounds rough? It is. Your family may complain about not being able to "do anything" in the house. This may be true. You may have to adjust what you and your family can do. If you can't keep up with the mud tracked in, you may have to go through the garage and remove your shoes outside the door. If the kitchen is always a mess, you may have to limit exactly who gets to get snacks and drinks and who doesn't. You may have to spend one day a week cooking, then cleaning up, and having ready-to-go meals stuck away in the refrigerator or freezer to help cut down on the cooking mess every day. You may want to eat out on the patio table if possible instead of in the dining room. Avoiding a mess in the first place is easiest.

If the family towels are a problem, you may want to put a rack or clothesline in the garage or basement and have everyone return their towel to that area to dry. If beds aren't getting made, you may have to get everyone up a few minutes earlier to get it done before they leave. And when you return from work and school, you may not be able to flop down in front of the television. Just ten or fifteen minutes may be enough to get your house in staged perfection, as long as everyone cooperates.

Yes, it's a tough assignment and one that never ends until the deal is done. You and your family are on task every day. Is it worth it? Yes. Because when a buyer shows up, your house (and you!) are ready.

Remember; it's all about the money at this point. Don't let a buyer walk away because they trip over boots in the hallway or must step over wet towels on the bathroom floor. Buyers are finicky because they can afford to be. Can you afford to be messy?

## The Beginning of The End

You have been through so many levels of physical and emotional turmoil, it's hard to imagine that someday it will all come to an end. But it will. And that's the beginning.

No matter what brought you to the decision to sell your house, you have taken it upon yourself to create the most value you can get out of your house. That was a big task. Each day you had to decide how deeply committed you were to this project. I know that many of these assignments took more time and effort than you had expected, or hoped. But, you did it.

You are ready now to let go and move on. These have been trying times. Now is the time to look forward and know that you've done everything you can to ensure a successful sale.

Whether you have listed your house with an estate agent, or are selling it yourself, make sure each buyer is treated as a guest in your home. Be ready for them and make them comfortable. Give them the room to roam. Be ready for their questions. That's your job now.

Then relax and wait for the offers to come rolling in. You've done everything you can to stage your house for a quick sale. You've removed as many obstacles as you could, so nothing is standing in the way. Your buyer will come when the time is right... and you will be ready for them!

Congratulations!

## About the author

Norah is Irish but has experience living and working in the UK, The Netherlands and New Zealand.

She lives in a 19th century cottage in the Sunny South East of Ireland with her rescue dog Barney and enjoys being close to her family again.

This is her third book and the second non-fiction work. Her books and short stories are available on Amazon.

Made in the USA
Middletown, DE
06 August 2017